Notes for the Goats® Presents

Self-Publishing MY Way

*A Beginner's Guide for Publishing Independently
without Leaving the Comfort of Your Home*

Amber Rose Bidmead

*This book is dedicated to all the independent
authors and first-time self-publishers.*

*Enjoy the creative process of birthing your book,
and may your words give life to dry bones!*

"What no spouse of a writer can ever understand is that a writer is working when he/she is staring out of the window."
- Burton Rascoe

Contents

1. Writing a Book 1
2. The Importance of a Title 4
3. Vanity Publishers 6
4. Finding an Editor 8
5. An Excellent Layout 10
6. Publishing Company 13
7. Purchasing an ISBN 16
8. LCCN 17
9. Copyrights 18
10. Works Cited and Bibliography 20
11. Endorsements 21
12. POD 22
13. Books in Print: Main Directory 25
14. Formatting an eBook 26
15. The Real Work Begins 28
16. Online Social Networking 30
17. Slow and Steady 33

"Writing is the only thing that when I do it, I don't feel I should be doing something else."
-Gloria Steine

Introduction

Ever since I published my first book, countless people continue to ask me how I do it and if I would mind helping them do the same. Honestly, I would love to help everyone, but it would take time away from doing what I'm most passionate about, which is writing my own books. So, what's a writer to do? You got it! Write a book about it!!

My book is not the only way to self-publish, but it is MY Way for those interested. It is a basic, informative guide that will successfully point writers in the right direction on their self-publishing journey. I wish I would have had a book like this when I started out!

It's my way of giving *new*, independent authors a helping hand. Now, when people ask 'how', I can direct them here. We both win!

There is a great sense of accomplishment when you publish your first book and an even greater sense of excitement knowing you did it on your own. I always find the creative process very rewarding. I'm excited to share with you the nuggets of wisdom I've found along this journey!

"I admire anybody who has the guts to write anything at all."
-E. B. White

Writing a Book

"Writing comes more easily if you have something to say."
-Sholem Asch

Writing a book is an exciting task! It's a roller coaster of emotions and stressors, but nonetheless exciting! I feel things I've never felt before (good and bad), but once accomplished, the joy of birthing my baby – I mean book – is amazing! It's worth the pain of labor!

Your book is your pride and joy. It's a child you are helping grow up to be everything it was meant to be. The connection you form with your book is one only an author can understand. It can be a sweet honeymoon romance or a bitter break- up. It is definitely a love-hate relationship. At times, you write pages without coming up for air, while other times it's neglected for months on end, but it's yours. You slowly breathe life into it with every word you type. Your book is part of you. This is why it is so hard to hear any negative input, even when it is meant with good intentions.

People write for all sorts of reasons. Some writers are artists; they write with beauty and grace – creating a world of words the way a painter would on a canvas. Others write because they have something to say; they aren't writing to show off their amazing skills or to even create a new world for the reader. Writing, in essence, is their microphone. It's their pulpit. We are all different, yet the same.

When starting your book, think about the type of writer you are. What are your strengths, and what are your challenges? What is the purpose behind your writing? What is the end goal? Keep in mind that this can change for each book you write.

It is important to be authentic when writing your book. Write with conviction. When people try to be like other writers, they are not being authentic to themselves or the gift they've been given. Young writers will often cling to authors they admire and try to mimic them. Have courage to embrace your own writing style, say what is in your heart, and be true to the words life has given you.

As a Christian writer, it would be easy for me to try to be like Beth Moore, Rick Warren, or – God forbid – C.S. Lewis. I have noticed that many Christian authors aspire to be the next Lewis, and this is a shame. C.S Lewis was who God created him to be during his time, and we should do the same in our time.

Having courage is the key to being a great writer. You must have the courage to be different – the courage to say what hasn't been said – the courage to ruffle a few feathers – the courage to stand alone – the courage to put your heart out there for all to see. It doesn't take courage or talent to be a copycat!

Be sure that whatever you are writing, no matter the genre, is something you believe in, something you're proud of, and something that adds more good to the world.

The Importance of a Title

A good title can launch a bad book, and a bad title can cripple a good book.

Try not to be self-indulgent when picking a title – really seek wisdom, think about your book, and come up with something catchy, clever, and interesting.

Don't rush into it and choose the first title you think of. Make a list and "sleep on it". It's interesting how much our opinions can change after a good night's sleep. The titles of my books usually "pop up" as I'm writing the book. They are usually sentences or parts of sentences that I've already written in the heat of a good writing moment. Some of them, on the other hand, I just *know*. It's as if they were supernaturally placed within me. Have you had that happen?

Once you've picked a great title, you may want to protect it. If you plan to use it in a series or as a brand, you'll want to get it trademarked. When I'm ready to do this, I contact a lawyer to have him fulfill this task. It is pretty pricey, so be sure it's something you really feel needs protecting. Some people try filing the information on their own through the following government website: www.uspto.gov. Be sure to read the directions carefully, or you may need to start over! Also, if you plan to do this, then begin early, as it can take several months to process.

The title is usually the first thing people will read when viewing your book. Would you pick up a book with your title? Don't be afraid to "test the waters" and ask for honest opinions from a few people you trust. Remember, they are going to be your future buyers. While their opinions aren't the only determining factors, they should certainly help with your decision-making!

Vanity Publishers

V anity Publishers. Agh! Every self-publisher should be wary of these companies, and it would be negligent of me to not mention this.

Vanity publishers are companies that offer to publish, edit, and market an author's book for a fee. It looks good on the outside (depending upon how high the fee), but a closer look will show that these companies make the majority of their money from the up-front fees – not from selling your book – which means no money for you!

Also, if your book does sell, they take a large percentage of the royalties. It's better to take the time to edit, design, and find a print-on-demand (POD) company on your own. (I discuss each of these in later chapters).

When I was writing my first book, I came across several vanity publishing companies. They sounded great! I even began exchanging emails with one of the companies, seeking more information about its services.

This particular company almost had me until I saw the up-front fees (which I could not afford) and the fact that I couldn't design my own layout or cover. I would be handing over all creative input!

As a creative individual, that bothered me! I wanted to be more hands-on.

I also didn't believe their sales plan was executed very well. It appeared that they were more interested in pumping out hundreds of books from whomever, rather than publishing quality books and focusing on selling them to their best ability. I didn't want to be *just* another book to them. My book was special! Your book is special!

A true publishing company will not ask you to pay an up-front fee. They make money from selling YOUR book! Companies that ask for up-front fees are doing so because they aren't making money from book sales!

Don't fall for it! You can do what they do AND keep the rights, have creative input, and earn more royalties!

By the end of this book, you will know how!

Finding an Editor

"You write to communicate to the hearts and minds of others what's burning inside you. And we edit to let the fire show through the smoke." - Arthur Polotnik

It's important to find a good editor. I've been truly blessed in this area. I love my editor! She has a true editing gift and is full of passion for what she does!

When searching for an editor, it's best to select someone who is excited about the job. If there is a lack of enthusiasm, this is a "red flag"! You don't want someone doing a so-so job by carelessly flipping through the pages of your book. You want them to be full of energy about the assignment. This book is your baby! Choose the best!

Anyone can create a uniform look for your book, but a true editor is good with words and punctuation. You want someone who will transform your book into a smooth read without editing out the book's personality.

It's sad that a few typos can ruin your book's influence, but it is a reality. As a writer, when I see typos in a book, I have compassion for the author because I know how tedious and monotonous editing a book can be. By the time a book is published, the author is usually sick of his/her own book because of having read it a million times forward and backward and every which way. After a while, all the words begin to read the same and become a blur.

It's like a mother when she is getting closer to her due date. She just wants the baby out! She's tired of being pregnant! Then, once the baby is in her arms, the last few weeks of misery are forgotten… or so I'm told.

Can you relate? This sounds strangely familiar – as it is exactly how I'd describe my experience with publishing my first book! When I finally held the first manifested copy of my book, though, it was the most incredible feeling. It was surreal!

My hours-upon-hours of hard work had paid off!! Yours will, too!

Don't cut corners!

An Excellent Layout

Visual appeal is everything! If your book is not visually appealing, you risk losing credibility with your readers. A sloppy layout equals a sloppy mind... or something like that! People may not show it, but in their hearts you've lost them. In order to sell books, you need influence. Why risk losing influence over something as easy and fun to fix as your layout?

I suggest finding books that you visually love. Think about why you enjoy the looks, and learn from them. Look for books you find to be sloppy, and learn from them as well. That's what I do! Pay attention to the details – everything from the set-up of the table of contents, page numbers, book size, and margin spacing – it all matters!

During the publishing process, you will learn a lot about Microsoft Word. You can search your questions online and even watch YouTube videos on how to perform certain tasks. It's worth the research time if it helps the over-all appearance of your book.

For example, when I published my first book, it was difficult trying to figure out how to use Roman numerals as my page numbers for the acknowledgment, foreword, and introduction pages and then switching back to regular numbers when my chapters began. How on earth was I going to get page 1 to start on page 20? It took some research on my part, but it was worth the professional look. Details matter! Go the distance! As your own publisher, you will need to learn to search out answers. Your book is depending upon you.

Another critical aspect of the layout is your book cover. Think about your key audience. Is it male, female, or both? Keep this in mind while designing and choosing images. If your book is intended for both male and female, you may not want to put a bouquet of flowers on the cover. Could you see a guy holding it? Yea, neither could he! You just lost a customer! Is your book for females? Play that up by making a feminine cover. Also think about the age range of your audience. Could you see an elderly person holding your book? What about a teen or a child? Considering your audience is a vital step toward success. Do not accidentally narrow your appeal! Design for the appropriate audience!

Also, ask for opinions. I remember trying a number of different pictures for my book cover, but each was "shot down" by people I care about. We engaged in arguments over it because I was sure I had finally found a winner, and I was extremely sensitive about it. I learned, though, that it is worth listening to other people's perspectives, as there are usually legitimate concerns and ideas. *They* are the people buying your book! Ask, and then listen!

Ugly may sell once, but it usually won't sell twice. Meaning – someone may buy your first book, but if it looks sloppy, the same person probably won't buy your second book. As self-publishers, we cannot afford to lose customers in that fashion. We build our platform by winning people over with each and every book, carrying our fans with us year after year.

Publishing Company

This step was somewhat tricky for me because I didn't know it was a step until it "slapped" me in the face!

You need to create a publishing company in order to get your ISBNs (International Standard Book Numbers) and your LCCNs (Library of Congress Catalog Numbers). While you may opt out of having these assigned numbers, I would not recommend it. Without them, your book will be as a "lone ranger", wandering the wilderness – lost and alone – and basically be non-existent in the world of books.

You may be wondering, *"Can I pay a company to assist me in attaining these numbers?"*

If you haven't created a publishing company, then yes, you can pay a company to assist you. However, the numbers will always be associated with that company. As an independent author and "want-to-be" self-publisher, you want the numbers associated with you, or at least I do! Think about it – what you are actually doing is a publishing operation! Why not set yourself up as the official publisher?

Once you have named your publishing company, check online resources to avoid company name duplication.

Then, when you are ready to purchase your ISBNs and LCCNs, complete the form as the official publisher, using the name you've chosen and your personal address or P.O.Box.

Now, you may be saying, *"Yippee! I can start my own publishing company and publish others' books, too!"*, and you can, but you need to decide what you would rather do – publish or write?

After you've published your first *quality* book (quality being the key word), you will have a good idea of about how much work it takes. Can you really publish other people's books in addition to writing and publishing your own? I'm guessing some people do, but it's very difficult to do both well, unless you hire a team of people to do most of the legwork. Even with that, though, unless you can produce huge sales, you will probably end up being just another vanity publishing company – so be careful.

Also, as you will soon see, the hardest part of self-publishing doesn't come into play until AFTER your book is published. If you can make your own self-published book successful, then and *only* then, do I recommend publishing other people's books. If you can't get your own book off the ground, what makes you think you can market someone else's? It involves a lot of blood, sweat, and tears that are better spent promoting your own books!

Purchasing an ISBN

What is an ISBN? An ISBN is an "International Standard Book Number". Every sellable book needs one! I recommend buying a block of numbers. In order to buy a block, you will have needed to have created a publishing company (as discussed in the previous chapter). Your block of ISBN numbers can be purchased at www.MyIdentifiers.com.

When purchasing your ISBN block, you will also be asked to purchase a barcode. This is unnecessary if you've chosen a POD (print on demand) company that provides a barcode for you. My POD source is a company called "CreateSpace", and it generates the necessary barcodes for me. When it comes to using my own ISBN when uploading my book, I simply follow the steps provided. (I explain more about this in the chapter entitled "POD".)

LCCN

An LCCN is the "Library of Congress Catalog Card Number" and is a pre-assigned card number (PCN) that appears on the copyright page of a book. It's important to apply for an LCCN if you would like for your book to be available in libraries. It is absolutely free and can be ordered for a book having more than 50 pages. Once your book is printed, you will need to mail a hard copy to the Library of Congress.

You can learn more about LCCNs and the application process by visiting the Library of Congress's website: www.loc.gov.

I recommend applying for one. Again, it adds to the professional quality of your book.

Copyrights

Some authors inadvertently forget to add a copyright page to the front of the book! This is another reason it's important to look at a well-published book for wisdom, just as you did for your layout. Whatever a well-published book has included, ask yourself why and how, then do the same! The more professional your book looks, the better!

The copyright page can look overwhelming at first glance, but if you break it down, it's not so bad.

The top half of the copyright page is all about you and your book: the title, your copyrights, your publishing company, trademark information, and contact information.

You can attain an official copyright for your book by going to www.copyright.gov.

On the bottom half of your copyright page, is the list of people involved in the publishing of your book, such as editors, co-writers, and those who gave creative input. Next are your ISBN and LCCN numbers.

Sound exhausting? Yes, there is a lot of legwork for a self-publisher, but again, it's worth it!

You may have been thinking you would jump in "head first" publishing your own books and other folks' books on top of that! Whew!

Works Cited and Bibliography

A works cited page and reference page both refer to the same page. It's a page where you list all the works you have cited or referenced in your book. I recommend doing this as you go. Don't wait until you are finished with your book to recall everyone you've cited.

A bibliography page, on the other hand, is not the same. This page is dedicated to works you have used for research but didn't actually cite in your book. It's important to understand the difference.

As you flip through other books, you will see a lot of variations on how to set up these pages. Some authors make a reference page in the back of the book, some at the end of every chapter. It is up to you, but give credit where credit is due. It's the law.

Also, ask permission to use other published information before doing so. Most books will have a publisher listed. The publisher's website will state *how much* information and *what* information is allowed to be quoted.

There are many online resources to help you construct these pages. There are even some that will make a works cited list for you when you type in a book's ISBN number. Awesome!

Endorsements

Endorsements will add credibility to your book. Don't be afraid to ask influential people you know to read and endorse your book. You may get "shut-down" a few times, but a few yes's are worth a few no's. Endorsements are usually placed on the very first few pages of your book and on the back cover. While it's certainly a great bonus to have endorsements, try not to be discouraged if you are unable to get any.

I also encourage you to find someone with some level of influence to write a foreword for your book. Again, this is not necessary, but it adds credibility.

As a self-publisher, it is your job to make your book as professional as possible. You can do it!

POD

POD means "print on demand", and it's a self-publisher's best friend! Gone are the days when authors must buy hundreds of thousands of their own books – filling their homes, hallways, and car trunks – fronting money they don't have. Times have changed for the self-publisher's benefit!

Once you've written your book and accomplished all the steps described in previous chapters, it is time for you to begin thinking about how to actually produce copies of your book. You can pay some off-the-wall publishing company to do it, as I mentioned in the chapter, "vanity publishers" (not a good idea), or you can pay a printing company to produce boxes-upon-boxes of your books that you must then figure out how to sell. Better yet, just do what I do! Use a POD company!

A POD company will host your book, allowing people to buy it online, and then ship the book directly to the customer. After that, the company will mail you a check for the amount of your profit! It's easy! And you don't have to front a bunch of money and hoard boxes of your books in every corner of your house. The book is produced and shipped only when someone buys it!

After much research, I have chosen CreateSpace (an Amazon company), as my POD source. I believe it by far offers the best services and allows you to keep ALL the rights to your book. (At least it did when I wrote this, so be sure to double-check!) It's important that before choosing any company to work on your baby – I mean book – you thoroughly read the fine print. Imagine the following scenario: You self-publish, and a few years later you get picked up by a major publisher. Then, when trying to take your book back from your POD source, you find that you can't – all because you didn't read the fine print – and the previous company owns your book and title! Scary?! It's like a babysitter refusing to give back your child! READ THE FINE PRINT!! Be sure that you keep the rights to your book.

I love CreateSpace for many reasons! The site is user-friendly, and the customer service is great! (I really should get paid for advertising the company like this – Ha-Ha! It's okay, though, because I can't lie – I really love it!) The amount of service provided is extremely helpful. There is a cover maker for authors not having a book cover, and there are numerous other services to benefit from. You'll even find information to guide first-time publishers. For example, there is a section about industry standards and what is accepted for different sales outlets. When I first started out, I had no clue about some of that stuff!! The company even provides ISBN numbers and barcodes for people without them.

Another benefit I've found with CreateSpace is the amount of royalties an author receives. It offers the highest. Also, there are no up-front costs. Creating an account and downloading your book is a free service through CreateSpace! The company does take a cut from your royalties, but that's to be expected for the printing and shipping of your book! The cut is far less than that of other publishing companies from what I've discovered.

If you're new to the world of publishing, you may have the misconception that an author of a book gets paid the amount the customer pays for the book, but that is far from the truth. In most cases, an author's profit is much less than the book's asking price.

As you can see, there are many reasons as to why I selected CreateSpace for my POD source. There are a number of other great companies available as well, but do your research, read the fine print, and choose a company that fits you best.

Books in Print: Main Directory

When your book is ready to meet the public, you will need to register it with *Books in Print* at www.Bowkerlink.com. *Books in Print* is the main directory for books! From bookstores to libraries and all kinds of online retailers – they ALL use *Books in Print* to find books for their customers (soon to be *your* customers). You will receive more information about registering your book with *Books in Print* when you order your ISBNs.

Formatting an eBook

This chapter is the perfect example of why I love CreateSpace! I simply sent the company an email asking about formatting my already-uploaded book into a Kindle acceptable file, and this POD company did it! It took several weeks to complete, but it was beautifully done!

Then, I opened an Amazon account by clicking the link *"Independently Publish With Us"* at the bottom of the website. Next, I clicked on *"Kindle Books"* on the left side of the page and uploaded my eBook.

Formatting an eBook is torture, or at least it is for me, so paying someone else to do it is my recommendation!

Now, if you want to upload your book and sell it on iBooks, you may need to go through a third party, like SmashWords, depending upon your computer. That's what I do.

It's vital that you get your book formatted as an eBook. More people are buying books online with their Kindles, Nooks, and iPads. Hardback and soft-covered books are quickly becoming a thing of the past. Book stores are closing down across the nation! If you want your book to have a chance at being successful, it must be available as an eBook!

The Real Work Begins

Finally!! Your book is published! It's time to party, right?!?! Wrong! Pop the balloons, and toss out the cake!

Everything to this point was as easy as it's going to get! The real work has just begun!

Creating an author platform and promoting your book can be a nightmare task. The truth is that not many people are reading books nowadays, and trying to convince someone to buy your book without a huge manipulative marketing team backing you up is hard and almost impossible!!

I could write a bunch of encouraging "stuff" in this section, but the truth is that this is the hardest part of self-publishing – advertising and marketing. This phase certainly brings to light one of the biggest advantages of signing with a big publishing house. If you are extremely concerned about the sales of your book, then you will find yourself very frustrated at this stage, especially if you don't already have a platform of some sort (speaker, teacher, pastor, etc.).

For those who have a bit of influence already, self-publishing is definitely the route to take, as you are in control of yourself and your product, and since you already have a following, selling should not be as hard for you. Also, remember that as a self-publisher, you make a higher percentage of royalties.

If you don't have influence or a following, then this will be a slow process, but it can be done! Don't lose hope!

The key is online social networking!

Online Social Networking

Face it! Where are most people spending their time? Where are most people buying things? Where are your customers?

ONLINE!!

The more places online you create a platform, the better!

Online Social Networking is the most important asset for a self-publisher! Please do NOT overlook this! Social Networking is your second best friend (next to a POD company). You need the following:

Website

Every self-publisher needs a website. A website is a place where people can find out more about you and your product. It's where all your other platforms should refer back to. The key is to lead traffic to your website through your other networking sites.

Blog

Yes, you need a blog! A blog shows a customer that you are "real". It's a place to post fresh ideas and thoughts, and it helps to keep your customers "in the loop". It allows people to get to know you on a personal level, but don't get *too* personal! You don't want to lose influence! Keep it professional by staying focused on your genre of writing and your key audience.

Facebook Fan Page

A Facebook fan page is another great asset for self-publishers. It is where you can collect fans in one place, notify them of upcoming events, and again, direct them back to your website/product. Facebook fan pages also have neat tools that allow you to post a live news feed on your website. This means that your Facebook fan page updates can be seen on your website and blog.

YouTube

Creating a YouTube account allows you to make online commercials for your book using even the most basic movie-maker programs. It also allows you to talk to your fans personally. This may not be for everyone, but remember, the more places you engage online, the more people you have access to.

Twitter

The best tool yet! Twitter has more beneficial uses for a self-publisher than Facebook and blogs combined! It allows you to build your brand and reputation while connecting with thousands of people in and out of your field.

These are only five of the main networking sites I use! There are tons of others that you can benefit from as well! It can be overwhelming when considering all the possibilities, so I recommend just focusing on these five at first. You can always add others later.

Once you've created online platforms, consider connecting them onto your phone so that you can quickly and easily update all your sites. It's possible to even connect them in a way that your Twitter update becomes your Facebook update and vice-versa! Many blog sites even allow you to update your blogs from your mobile phone. The world is changing!!

I do most of my online networking from my phone, and not plopped down in front of a computer. Thank God for that, because after spending several hours a day writing, I truly don't feel like spending more time in front of the computer! I love being able to connect with people by simply using my phone, whether I'm at the gym, shopping with friends, or visiting my family.

Slow and Steady

Once you've accomplished all that is in this book, and your books have been successfully published for several months, you may find yourself a little discouraged about the harvest. The truth is that being an independent author is a slow and steady race. It's not a sprint to the finish line. Building an author platform and spreading the word about your book(s) is not an overnight success story most of the time. It takes time, effort, and persistence.

Continue looking for opportunities to market your book(s). Again, think about your audience. Where do they spend their time? What do they read? Advertise in these places. If you are on a budget (as most of us are), consider the online places in which you'll find your audience. The more online presence you have, the more hits your website will receive. Be creative when it comes to marketing. Consider investing in a few good marketing books to help inspire new ideas.

Most importantly – keep moving forward. One book at a time, you will build a successful platform.

"If I fall asleep with a pen in my hand, don't remove it - I might be writing in my dreams." - Terri Guillemets

Contact Information and Resources
NotesForTheGoats.com